Apple Action!

By Erin Benoit   Pictures by Chris Lensch

Dedicated to all the early childhood
teachers who use creativity and sense of
humor to make learning fun for children.
E. B.

First published by Experience Early Learning Company
7243 Scotchwood Lane, Grawn, Michigan 49637 USA

ISBN: 978-1-937954-44-4
Visit us at www.ExperienceEarlyLearning.com

Apple Action!

By Erin Benoit   Pictures by Chris Lensch

I'm an apple,
I grew on a tree,
There are so many things
you can do with me!

Are you ready?
Here we go!
We'll have fun
from head to toe.

I'm oh so crisp
and sometimes red...
Can you balance me
on your head?

I grew big
and round on a farm…
Can you tuck me
under your arm?

My shape is a sphere
and I'm always 3D…
Can you try
jumping over me?

I'm not a pear
and I'm surely not a date...
Can you lift me
like a weight?

I'm not a plum
and I'm not a prune…
Can you point me
to the moon?

14

I'm a tasty fruit
but I'm so much more…
Can you roll me
across the floor?

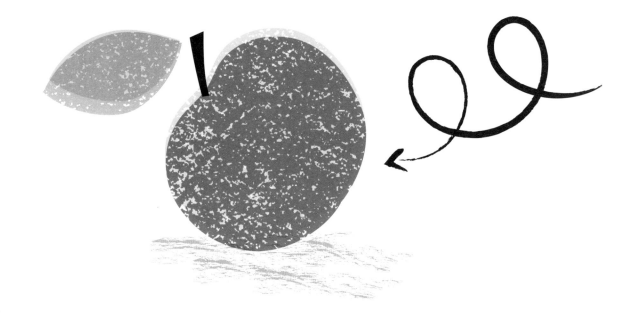

I'm a tough little fruit
but please handle with care…
Can you toss me
into the air?

I hang on a branch,
and that's where I grow.
Can you place me
on top of your toes?

My apple friends,
we all come from trees…
Can you hold me
between your knees?

I have a star,
it's quite a sight…
Go ahead
and take a (pretend) bite!

You did a great job!
Now take a bow...

Can you choose
where I go now?

The End